Hero or Villain?

Claims and Counterclaims

Geronimo

Leader of Native American Resistance

Jeri Freedman

Cavendish Square
New York

Published in 2019 by Cavendish Square Publishing, LLC
243 5th Avenue, Suite 136, New York, NY 10016

First Edition

Website: cavendishsq.com

Library of Congress Cataloging-in-Publication Data

Names: Freedman, Jeri, author.
Title: Geronimo : leader of Native American resistance / Jeri Freedman.
Description: First edition. | New York : Cavendish Square, 2018. |
Series: Hero or villain?: claims and counterclaims | Includes bibliographical references and index. |
Audience: Grade 7 to 12.
Identifiers: LCCN 2017061186 (print) | LCCN 2017061789 (ebook) |
ISBN 9781502635334 (eBook) | ISBN 9781502635327 (library bound) |
ISBN 9781502635341 (pbk.) Subjects: LCSH: Geronimo, 1829-1909--Juvenile literature. |
Apache Indians--Kings and rulers--Biography--Juvenile literature. | Apache Indians--Wars--Juvenile literature.
Classification: LCC E99.A6 (ebook) | LCC E99.A6 F84 2018 (print) |
DDC 979.004/97250092 [B] --dc23
LC record available at https://lccn.loc.gov/2017061186

Editorial Director: David McNamara
Editor: Michael Spitz
Copy Editor: Rebecca Rohan
Associate Art Director: Amy Greenan
Designer: Amy Greenan/Christina Shults
Production Coordinator: Karol Szymczuk
Photo Research: J8 Media

The photographs in this book are used by permission and through the courtesy of:
Cover Everett Historical/Shutterstock.com; p. 4 Hulton Archive/Getty Images; p. 5 (used throughout the book) Wikimedia Commons/File:Cantino planisphere (1502).jpg/Public Domain; p. 6 De Agostini Picture Library/Getty Images; p. 9 © CORBIS/Corbis via Getty Images; p. 10 Leemage/UIG via Getty Images; p. 12 Sopotnicki/Shutterstock.com; p. 21 Margaret Duncan Coxhead/Wikimedia Commons/ File:ROHM D237 Conquistadors exhort their supporters.jpg; p. 24 © North Wind Picture Archives; p. 25 Published in the 1851 book "The War Between the United States and Mexico, Illustrated"./Wikimedia Commons/File:Mexico nebel.jpg; p. 27 North Wind Picture Archives/Alamy Stock Photo; p. 30 Rochester Historical Society/Wikimedia Commons/File:Overland Mail Station Arthur Lee.jpg; p. 33 National Archives American West Photographs/Wikimedia Commons/File:Shoshone indians.jpg; p. 34 Denver Post via Getty Images; p. 40 The Making of America: Apache Country!, McBride, Angus (1931- 2007) /Private Collection/ © Look and Learn/Bridgeman Images; p. 44 Science History Images/Alamy Stock Photo; p. 47 Time Life Pictures/National Archives/The LIFE Picture Collection/Getty Images; p. 48 Popperfoto/Getty Images; p. 53 Universal History Archive/UIG via Getty Images; p. 56 GraphicaArtis/Getty Images; p. 60 Leemage/Corbis via Getty Images; p. 64 World History Archive/Alamy Stock Photo; p. 6 Billy Hathorn/Wikimedia Commons/File:ATSF Rail car in Hereford, TX IMG 4861. JPG; p. 69 Library of Congress/Corbis/VCG via Getty Images; p. 76 PawełMM/Wikimedia Commons/File:Theodore Roosevelt shaking hands from a train photograph restored.jpg; p. 79 Cowan's Auctions/Wikimedia Commons/ File:Capture and Death of Sitting Bull by Kurz & Allison, 1890.jpg; p. 86 Ralph Crane/The LIFE Picture Collection/Getty Images; p. 90-91 ScreenProd/Photononstop/Alamy Stock Photo; p. 94 Museum of Science and Industry, Chicago/Getty Images; p. 96 Ralph Crane/The LIFE Picture Collection/Getty Images.

Printed in the United States of America

CONTENTS

Geronimo is one of the most famous and controversial Native Americans.

Geronimo and the Changing Southwest

Chapter One

Geronimo was a Bedonkohe Apache. The Bedonkohe Apache lived in the upper Gila Valley in Arizona. Born in 1829, his birth name was Goyahlkla, which means, "one who yawns." "Geronimo" was a nickname he was given as a warrior. Geronimo grew to manhood in the final days of Mexican rule of the region that would become the American Southwest. He is viewed by some people as a leader of Native American resistance against the Mexicans and Americans who were claiming the land that the Apache had lived on for generations. Not only was the settlement of Native American lands done without regard for their rights or welfare, but the process disrupted the Apaches' way of life and endangered their ability to survive. Other people view Geronimo as a ruthless killer who attacked not only military forces, but also civilians. He was a man who solved problems with violence and was unwilling to compromise.

A Time of Change

In the time that Geronimo lived, the ownership of the land in the Southwest was in flux. In 1846, the Mexican and American governments both claimed ownership of the territory north of the Rio Grande. The result was the Mexican-American War. In 1848, two events occurred that affected Geronimo and the Apache. In February 1848, Mexico surrendered and signed the Treaty of Guadalupe Hidalgo, ceding to the United States territories a total of 500,000 square miles (1.3 million square kilometers), including Arizona and New Mexico. Later that year, the discovery of gold in the Southwest led a large number of miners and settlers to move into the region. The establishment of mines, ranches, and towns in Arizona disrupted the free-roaming life of the Apache because the colonists attempted to set

General Winfield Scott's troops attacked Chapultepec Castle in Mexico during the Mexican-American War.

limits on where and how the Apache could live. The Apache naturally objected. Geronimo led the Apache in resistance to the white colonization of the lands where the Apache lived in the Southwest. He also conducted raids in Mexico. He and his followers killed Mexicans, whom he hated because the Mexican military had killed his family.

Betrayal and Revenge

In 1872, Cochise, chief of the Chiricahua Apache, made a deal with the US government that an Apache reservation would be established on traditional Apache land. Three years later, Cochise died, and the US government immediately repudiated the agreement and moved the Apache north to barren desert land in San Carlo, Arizona. Although it was established as a reservation for the Chiricahua Apache tribe, various other Apache bands were forced from their lands and moved to the San Carlo reservation to make room for American settlers on the more desirable land. This betrayal infuriated Geronimo. He led the Apache on a new round of attacks.

Despite their best efforts, the US Army was unable to capture Geronimo for years. He was an expert in attacking and escaping to hide in the mountains. He was finally captured in 1877 and sent to live on the Apache reservation, but he and his followers repeatedly escaped and returned to attacking the invaders of their people's lands. Geronimo's repeated escapes embarrassed US politicians and army officers, and angered and terrified the white population. The newspapers, however, loved him for the dramatic copy he provided as they reported on his daring exploits. People

The Apache

The Apache are a group of related Native American tribes that originally lived in the Southwestern United States, including Eastern Arizona, Northern Mexico, New Mexico, West Texas, and Southern Colorado. Culturally, the Apache are divided into various subtribes, including the Chiricahua and Bedonkohe, among others. The Apache had no centralized tribal organization. Small groups of Apache, called "bands," functioned independently in different locations, each with its own leader. Sometimes, several bands were united under one leader, who acted as chief. Chiefs were elected by the tribe's warriors. They did not inherit the position.

In Geronimo's time, the Apache were a nomadic people. They hunted and gathered food, moving from place to place. They didn't engage in agriculture regularly until they were forced to live on reservations. Their houses were made of brush and were easily assembled and disassembled. Because of their nomadic lifestyle, they made few crafts. Instead, they traded buffalo hides, tallow, meat, bones (which could be made into needles and scrapers for hides), and salt from the desert with the Pueblo natives in exchange for pottery, blankets, turquoise, corn, and other goods. Sometimes,

A group of Apache in the 1870s

they simply raided other Native American villages and plundered them for goods. Because of this behavior, they became known among the Pueblo villages by the name "Apachu," which means "the enemy." The Apache applied their well-honed raiding tactics against the Spanish in the sixteenth century, the Mexicans in the eighteenth century, and the US military and settlers in the nineteenth century.

The Apache tribes fought the invading Spanish and Mexican peoples for centuries, with the first raids occurring in the late seventeenth century. During the American-Indian wars in the nineteenth century, the US Army found the Apache to be fierce warriors and skillful strategists.

A newspaper illustration dramatizes the US cavalry pursuing Native American warriors.

repeatedly heard of his ability to avoid capture by the US military, which endowed him with an almost mystical aura.

In 1886, after years of battle, Geronimo finally surrendered to US troops, thus ending the last of the Indian Wars. Over the next several years, Geronimo and his people were moved from prison to prison, in Florida, Alabama, and then finally to Fort Sill in Oklahoma. He spent more than twenty years as a prisoner. Throughout that time, he remained a celebrity. People wanted to see the famous Native American warrior. He was escorted under guard to major expositions where the public could view him. In 1905, he attained a private audience with President Theodore Roosevelt. He tried, unsuccessfully, to get the president to allow his people to return to Arizona. That same year, he wrote his autobiography. In 1909, he was thrown from a horse and, after spending the night in the cold, became ill with pneumonia. He died six days later at the age of eighty.

Geronimo was a complex man. Those who followed him thought of him as a defender of Native Americans and their way of life. Others, including many Apache, believed that he was a stubborn reactionary, refusing to accept the inevitable and pointlessly endangering people. The Mexican and American military and civilians saw him as a bloodthirsty savage, killing indiscriminately. So who was the real Geronimo?

These ruins show the typical design of Pueblo cliff dwellings in the Southwest.

History of the American Southwest

Chapter Two

The Southwest comprises eight states: Arizona, California, Colorado, Nevada, New Mexico, Oklahoma, Texas, and Utah. The terrain varies throughout the region. Deserts, including the Mojave, Sonoran, and Chihuahuan Deserts, dominate the southern and western parts of the Southwest. The Colorado Plateau includes forested areas and areas consisting of mesas interspersed with canyons, the largest of which is the Grand Canyon. Although primarily desert, Arizona contains the White Mountains in the eastern part of the state and the Superstition Mountains east of Phoenix. The largest mountain range in the Southwest is the Rocky Mountains, and the two largest rivers are the Colorado River to the north and the Rio Grande, which forms the border between the US Southwest and Mexico.

Early History

The earliest inhabitants of the Southwest were Paleolithic hunter-gatherers who crossed the land bridge across the Bering Strait from Asia in approximately 9000 BCE and inhabited the area for several thousand years. Archeologists refer to them as the Clovis culture, because tools from this people were first discovered near Clovis, New Mexico. By 1000 BCE, the people of the Clovis culture were replaced by three major pre-Columbian Native American groups: the Ancestral Pueblo people (also called the Anasazi), the Hohokam, and the Mogollon. The term "pre-Columbian" is used to describe Native American peoples who lived in America before the arrival of Columbus in 1492. By 1000 BCE, Native Americans began to supplement their hunting and gathering with agriculture. Their major crop was maize (corn).

The Ancestral Pueblo people began settling in the northern region of the Southwest around 1500 BCE. Archeological evidence of this culture, dating from approximately 1500 BCE through the middle of the fifteenth century CE, has been found. The Mogollon culture can be traced to the eastern part of the region, starting in approximately 300 BCE. Eventually, they spread into Mexico. They first lived in pit houses, round constructions into which inhabitants descended via ladders. These would evolve into pueblos—aboveground complexes of buildings, which inhabitants still entered via a ladder in a hole in the roof. The pueblos were often built into the sides of cliffs.

After 1300 CE, the pre-Columbian cultures began to decline, and all had disappeared by the end of the fifteenth century. The reason for this is not clear. Experts have suggested various explanations, including severe drought and the encroachment of other peoples. Many Native American tribes trace their ancestry back to these cultural groups, which suggests that they may have been assimilated into the later cultures. The area that had been occupied by the Mogollon was taken over by the Apache, who were not genetically related to them. The Apache originally lived in northwest North America—including Alaska, the Pacific Northwest, and Western Canada—and some Apache continued to inhabit those areas when others migrated into the American Southwest, previously inhabited by the Mogollon. The migration took place between 1200 and 1500 CE. They settled throughout the Southwest, including New Mexico, Arizona, northern Mexico, western Texas, and Colorado.

In the 1700s, the Comanche, a larger and fiercer tribe, began expanding its territories into the western Great Plains, driving the Apache farther west into the mountain ranges of Arizona and New Mexico. The Apache adapted to the harsh terrain the Comanche drove them into, hunting in the mountains in the summer and in the lower valleys in the winter. They were primarily nomads, but they did grow small amounts of beans, corn, and melons to supplement their diet.

The Way of the Warrior

On one hand, the various Native American tribes often traded with each other. On the other, conflict over territory and resources was also common, long before the Europeans reached North America. When the Europeans began to colonize the Southwest, the reduction in land available for use by tribes caused intertribal conflict to increase.

Native Americans didn't organize into formal militias as Europeans did. The usual attack was an ambush on the enemy or hit-and-run raids, both carried out by a small group of warriors. Small raids did sometimes lead to large-scale clashes between tribes that resulted in the destruction of one tribe's village—and usually the killing of all its inhabitants. In many tribes, a young man needed to prove his prowess as a warrior in order to achieve political power or marry well. Anyone in the tribe could organize a war party, and the drive for respect and recognition meant that young warriors organized raiding parties frequently. Tribes often had both war chiefs, who were experienced warriors, and peace chiefs, who managed trading and negotiations with neighboring tribes. It was often against the interest of the peace chiefs to have parties of warriors organizing raids on neighboring tribes, so they tried to discourage young warriors from doing so. The advice of the peace chiefs was often ignored. When the Europeans settled the Southwest, the raiding parties attacked them as well. In general, the nomadic tribes such as the Apache were more violent than the more settled tribes like the Pueblo people, but even the Pueblo sometimes fought with their neighbors.

The scalping of killed and captured enemies was a common practice. Scalping was not limited to North America, but was done by tribal people worldwide. Hair was viewed as a sign of strength, as in the Biblical story of Samson, so removing it was a powerful symbol of defeat for the enemy. Sometimes, the entire scalp and hair was taken, but often only a small patch of hair was removed and carried back to the camp by a warrior. In the United States, the practice of scalping originated among the tribes of the East and spread to those of the West.

The European Arrival

Spanish missionaries, who were based in Mexico, were the first Europeans to explore the Southwest. In 1539, Marcos de Niza, a Jesuit Franciscan, led an expedition from Mexico City, passing through eastern Arizona. When he returned to Mexico City after a year, he told conquistador and explorer Francisco Vázquez de Coronado that he'd seen one of the legendary Seven Golden Cities of Cibola. His report led Coronado to lead an outrageously expensive expedition to the site described by de Niza, only to find an ordinary pueblo village. When de Niza first met the Apache in 1541, he described them as "proud, fierce, and independent, but gentle if left alone."

Coronado's expedition laid the groundwork for the Spanish to claim Mexico and what is now the American Southwest. The Apache suffered severe economic and political disruptions, first from the Spanish, then from the Comanche, and later by the United States government. The Apache were aware of the various explorations of the Spanish in the sixteenth century, but the Spanish didn't cause them any hardship until 1598. At that time, an expedition led by Juan de Oñate entered the Pueblo country of the upper Rio Grande River Valley, in what is now New Mexico. Oñate's goal was to establish a permanent Spanish colony, and by 1610, the town of Santa Fe was built. Because the nomadic Apache didn't have a permanent home where they could manufacture goods, they were dependent on trade with settled Native American tribes, such as the Pueblo people in New Mexico. Until the arrival of the Spanish, the Apache traded regularly with the Pueblo. The Apache brought buffalo robes and dried meat to the Pueblo and traded them for agricultural products and pottery. Once they had control, the Spanish began to confiscate the goods the Pueblo made for trade, thus making them unavailable for trade with the Apache.

Jesuit priest Eusebio Kino started several missions in the Santa Cruz River Valley from 1687 to 1691. In 1694, he went on to explore southern and central Arizona. By this time, the Spanish had established permanent settlements in New Mexico. Although the Pueblo people had carried out a few rebellions against the Spanish, many were more interested in trading with the settlers. By the eighteenth century, European exploration was being replaced by European exploitation. European governments began to encourage their citizens to establish settlements in the lands their explorers had discovered, so the monarchy could lay claim to those regions. The Spanish were no exception. Starting in 1732, the Spanish government began to issue land grants in Mexico and the American Southwest, and settlers began to arrive and establish colonies.

In 1768, the Spanish declared all their Spanish holdings in the West, including California and the Southwest, to be one large Spanish province called the Provincia de las Californias (the Province of California). For the next fifty years, the Spanish continued to rule the Southwest. In

1804, Spain created the provinces of Alta California and Baja California by dividing the Provincia de las Californias. Alta California included the area that would later become California, Nevada, Arizona, Colorado, Utah, and New Mexico. In 1821, Mexico achieved its independence from Spain. In 1824, Mexico developed a constitution that established the Alta California Territory, which included the same geographic area as the earlier Spanish province.

In 1803, President Thomas Jefferson negotiated the Louisiana Purchase, in which America bought the French holdings that extended the length of the Mississippi River from Wisconsin through Louisiana. This brought the young United States of America into direct contact with the Spanish holdings on the western side of the continent. In 1836, the people living in what would become the Republic of Texas revolted and won independence from Mexico.

Annexing the Southwest

The United States did not annex Texas after it won independence from Mexico in 1836, because Mexico threatened war if they did so. In 1844, President John Tyler began negotiations with the Republic of Texas, which resulted in a treaty of annexation. The treaty had to be ratified by Congress, but it was initially debated in the US Senate. Adding Texas to the United States would upset the balance between the slave states and the free states. Some senators feared it would incite Mexico to declare war on the United States, especially as Mexico had disputed the US claim and broken off relations with the United States over the issue. Shortly before the end of his term of office, Tyler enlisted the help of James Polk, the incoming president, and succeeded in getting Congress to pass a law admitting Texas to the Union. Texas became a state on December 29, 1845. Polk had campaigned on the concept of "manifest destiny." The term manifest destiny represented the belief that white Americans were destined to expand their civilization across the entire continent of North America. To accomplish this mission, they had to annex the territories on the western side of the continent.

Although relations between the United States and Mexico remained tense, Mexico didn't declare war. Buoyed by his success in annexing Texas, President Polk sent troops into disputed lands along the Rio Grande in July 1845. In November, he sent diplomat John Slidell to Mexico to arrange adjustments to the border between the United States and Mexico and to try to purchase California and New Mexico. The Mexican government was unreceptive, but Polk was not deterred. He sent the US Army under General Zachary Taylor to the mouth of the Rio Grande, which the state of Texas claimed was its southern boundary. Mexico, however, claimed that its border with the United States was the Nueces River, northeast of the Rio Grande. The Mexican government considered the presence of Taylor's army south of the Nueces River to be an act of war. In April 1846, Mexican troops advanced across the Rio Grande. Polk declared the Mexican advance to be an invasion of US soil. On May 11, 1846, President Polk asked Congress to declare war on Mexico. On May 13, 1846, the US Congress voted in favor of the president's request. The Southwest became embroiled in the Mexican-American War.

Spanish conquistadors clashed with indigenous peoples when they explored the Americas.

Only seventy-five thousand Mexican citizens inhabited the area north of the Rio Grande. US forces were able to take those lands with minimal resistance. At the same time, Taylor crossed the Rio Grande into Mexico proper and captured the city of Monterrey. The goal of the battle was to dishearten the Mexicans and force them into a truce. Taylor's capture of Monterrey succeeded in achieving this goal, and it gave the Americans grounds for eventually pulling back only as far as they wanted—to the Rio Grande—and declaring the Rio Grande to be the border between the United States and Mexico, thus laying claim to the territory that would become the American Southwest.

The Mexicans recruited experienced general Antonio López de Santa Anna to take control of the Mexican army. At the Battle of Buena Vista in February 1847, Santa Anna's troops were forced to retreat. Also in February 1847, US troops led by General Winfield Scott landed in Veracruz, a coastal city not far from Mexico City. They took the city and then advanced toward Mexico City. At every point where they met Mexican troops, they won. In September 1847, Scott successfully laid siege to Mexico City, forcing the Mexicans to surrender.

The war ended with the Treaty of Guadalupe Hidalgo on February 2, 1848. Under the terms of the treaty, the Rio Grande became the official border between the United States and Mexico. The United States gained control of all of what is now California, Nevada, and Utah. It also acquired most of Arizona and part of Colorado and New Mexico. The United States paid Mexico fifteen million US dollars (equivalent to $452 million today) and agreed to settle all claims of US citizens against Mexico. The treaty added an additional 525,000 square miles (1,359,744 square kilometers) to United States territory. The rest of Arizona, Colorado, and New Mexico were part of Texas at the time, and the United States absorbed these areas when it annexed Texas. The remaining areas of the Southwest became part of the United States when the US government acquired the southernmost portions of Arizona and New Mexico in the Gadsden Purchase in 1853, negotiated by James Gadsden, then ambassador to Mexico.

With the Mexican-American War over and the disputed Southwest firmly in its grasp, the US government turned its attention to making the West safe for white settlers. Beginning in the 1850s, the government installed forts across the Southwest and used the army as a peacekeeping force against the Native Americans. There were frequent skirmishes between the soldiers and the Native Americans.

The Great Migrations

In the 1840s, the West was thoroughly explored and mapped by explorers such as John C. Frémont and the Army Corps of Engineers, under the direction of the US government. The government wanted to settle the region in order to establish undisputed control over the territory. In this way, the United States could fend off claims from other countries, such as Britain.

The 1840s were a period of vast migrations of settlers from the east to the west. This is the era of the famed Oregon Trail,

Trails Through the Southwest

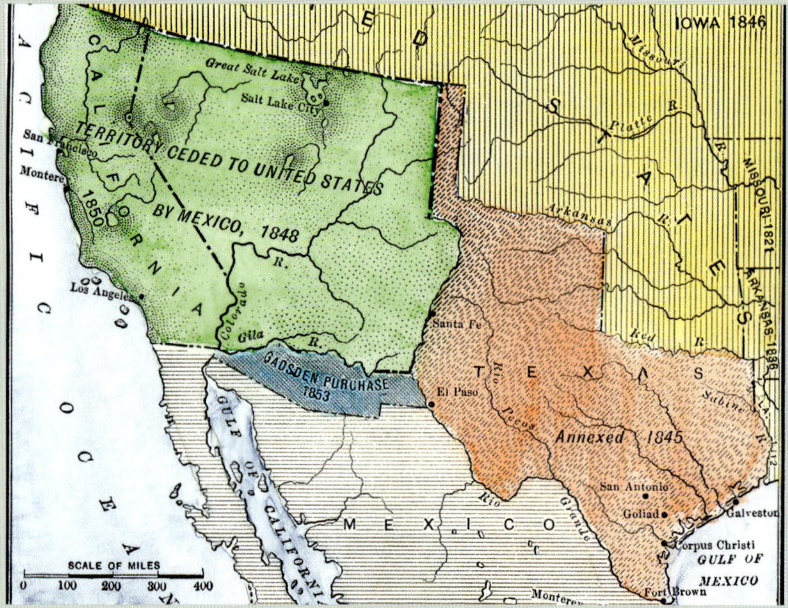

The Southwest United States from 1848 to 1853.

The discovery of gold in California in 1848 started a gold rush. It was necessary to cross the Southwest to reach California. Settlers and miners from the East and Midwest traveled along the Santa Fe and California Trails and streamed into Native American lands. Naturally, tensions mounted. The Apache stepped up their attacks, which included brutal ambushes on stagecoaches and wagon trains. The influx of settlers had a devastating effect on the native population. Settlers used up the resources in the region, such as wood, and killed the game, including the buffalo on which the Native Americans depended.

US troops invaded Mexico City during the Mexican-American War.

when thousands of travelers crossed the Rocky Mountains en route to the Oregon Territory. During the same period, the Mormons settled Utah, and thousands traversed the Southwest via the Santa Fe and California Trails on the way to the gold fields in California. In the 1850s, establishing transportation systems in the West became a major issue. Initially, large wagons were used to haul freight between the Midwest and the West. In 1869, the first transcontinental railroad was completed. The railroad was a 1,912-mile (3,077 km) connection between the eastern US rail network at the border of Omaha, Nebraska, and Council Bluffs, Iowa, and San Francisco Bay. The existence of the railroad made it much easier for people and goods to travel to and settle in the West.

In 1861, the Civil War began. Most of the major battles in the Civil War took place east of the Mississippi River, where most of the population of the United States resided. The largest effect that the war had on the Native American tribes was to deprive those on reservations of resources. The majority of troops were withdrawn from the West to fight in the East. The distribution of food and cash payments to Native American reservations was left in the hands of inexperienced local officials. The result was resources not arriving on time—or not arriving at all. This situation led to Native American uprisings across the West, all of which were eventually put down by the US Army forces sent to deal with them.

Once the Civil War ended in 1865, people turned their attention to homesteading and industry. The railroad and cheap land brought even more settlers to the West, and businessmen saw an opportunity to make money by providing goods and services to the settlers. These two factors brought huge numbers of people to the West. Most were white, but there were also ex-slaves looking for a new life and Chinese workers who had been brought in to build the railroad. More towns were established, and towns became cities. Conflict between the settlers and the Native Americans escalated.

The Apache Wars

Cochise was the chief of the Chiricahua Apache. He maintained a positive relationship with the Americans until the "Bascom Affair" of 1861. An uneasy standoff had developed between the Apache and the whites by the 1850s. There was great distrust between the Americans and

Covered wagons reach the end of the Santa Fe Trail in Santa Fe, New Mexico.

The Overland Mail Station, where the Bascom Affair took place

the process, they would cross through Apache Pass, where they could be seen by Apache scouts.

Mangas Coloradas was the head of the branch of the Apache to which Geronimo belonged. The bands of Cochise and Coloradas often fought as allies. The Cochise–Mangas Coloradas coalition did not intend to launch a full-out assault on the Overland Mail Station. When they saw the additional soldiers, they left. On February 14, more soldiers arrived. Searching the area, they encountered no Apache, but found the bodies of the American hostages. Given that the Apache appeared to have dispersed, the soldiers who had joined Bascom's troops departed. Bascom and three other officers met. Three of the officers wanted to hang the Apache captives in retaliation for the killing of the American hostages. Bascom alone objected, but he was overruled by his superior officer.

When the South announced it was seceding from the Union and forming the Confederacy, the Overland Mail Station was moved north. The moving of the Overland Mail Station didn't stop either Cochise's or Mangas Coloradas's Apache from taking revenge for the hanging of the Apache captives by killing workers who were trying to establish a mail route for the Confederacy and white travelers. They engaged in numerous attempts to drive the Americans from their territory. When Felix Ward grew up, he became what was then called an Indian agent, and he verified that it was not Cochise who had kidnapped him, but Apache from another tribe.

In the years following the Civil War, the success of the US troops in various battles between the US government and Native American tribes, in both the Plains and the West, had subdued most of the Native Americans. The last significant victory of the Native Americans occurred with the defeat of General Armstrong Custer at Little Big Horn in June 1876. The defeat of Chief Joseph and the Nez Perce in 1877 marked the end of Native American resistance in the West. The only holdouts that remained were the Apache in Arizona, led by Geronimo. The Apache Wars continued throughout the entire decade of the 1880s.

In 1874, Cochise, who had worked out peaceable solutions to relations with the Americans, died. Without Cochise's influence, the Apache dug in their heels against the whites who were destroying their way of life. At the same time, the Native Americans were exploited by the Tucson Group, a cartel of businessmen, army contractors, gunrunners, whiskey peddlers, and self-interested politicians.

Making the situation more incendiary was the US government's decision to lump together all the Apache tribes on the San Carlos reservation. The Apache were not one homogeneous tribe, and not all Apache tribes got along with each other. Putting them all together in a small space was a recipe for trouble. On several occasions, conflicts between groups of Apache resulted in bands leaving the reservation and returning to raiding. By the 1880s, westward expansion had created a great demand of land for both farming and ranching. In order to ensure the security of the white settlers, the government charged the US Army with killing any remaining Native Americans who refused to relocate to reservations.

American soldiers guard Native Americans on a reservation to ensure they do not escape.

A figure of the Chiricahua Apache leader Cochise

Geronimo and the American West

Chapter Three

To understand Geronimo's influence on the Apache, it is necessary to understand the distribution of power in Native American tribes. Apache tribal groups were not ruled by a single person. Instead, various individuals had responsibility for specific aspects of the community. There were village chiefs, war chiefs, peace chiefs, and a variety of other influential individuals. The people who held these positions of authority did so because they impressed the members of the tribe with their knowledge and skill in the area for which they were responsible. For example, Cochise, leader of the Chiricahua Apache, was a powerful peace chief who engaged in diplomacy with the federal forces in Arizona. He wished to achieve the best deals possible for his people without resorting to war.

Geronimo met his first white man in 1858, when he and some other warriors encountered some men who were surveying land. Although the Apache and surveyors couldn't talk to each other, they shook hands and made camps near each other. The Apache traded with the white men, giving them buckskins, blankets, and ponies in exchange for provisions and shirts. They brought the surveyors game that they had killed, which the men paid for with money. Geronimo had no idea what to do with the money, but he later showed it to some Navajo, who explained that it was valuable.

Personal Tragedy

Shortly after he met the white men in 1858, a young Geronimo (still called by his birth name, Goyahlkla) was on a regular trading trip with other warriors, walking from their territory to the neighboring Mexican state of Chihuahua. He was accompanied by his family, which consisted of his wife, his widowed mother, and three children, one being a baby carried on his wife's back. The group brought animal hides, wild herbs, and items they had acquired by raids in Mexico, which they planned to trade for knives, dyed cloth, beads, and the alcoholic beverage mescal.

The group decided to pitch camp near the town of Janos in northern Chihuahua. The women set up the camp, and the men loaded up the trade goods and went into the town. Only two warriors stayed behind to guard the camp. The men were successful in trading in Janos. As they approached the camp on the way back, they were intercepted by a small number of women and children. The distraught women informed them that the camp had been attacked by Mexican troops, who had come from the adjacent Mexican state of Sonora. After killing the guards, the Mexican soldiers had massacred all the women and children they could find. Only those who had escaped to the hills and hidden there had survived. After killing everyone, the troops had taken all their supplies and ponies.

Geronimo entered the camp. He found that his entire family had been killed. Mangas Coloradas, the chief of the band, declared that since they numbered only eighty warriors, were surrounded by Mexicans, and lacked adequate weapons, they should leave the dead and return home. Geronimo, in shock, stood by the nearby river as the others left. Finally, Mangas Coloradas collected him and they followed the rest of the band. When he reached his home village a few days later, he burned his wife and children's possessions and even the teepee they'd occupied. The murder of his family changed his life. In his autobiography, he wrote: "I was never again contented in our happy home, and whenever I saw anything to remind me of former happy days my heart would ache for revenge on Mexico." As a warrior, Geronimo had participated in raids against Mexicans since his teen years. The rage that filled him after the killing of his family infused him with an incredible fierceness and drive that would lead to his achieving a reputation as a warrior of tremendous determination and power.

Wishing to be alone with his grief, Geronimo headed into the wilderness to mourn. He was sitting alone and crying when he heard a voice. It said: "No gun will ever kill you. I will take the bullets from the guns of the Mexicans so they will have nothing but powder, and I will guide your arrows." He interpreted the voice as being that of Usen, the god of the Apache. The prediction turned out to be true. Geronimo would be wounded eight times, but he was not killed. During his time as a war leader, he was shot in the right leg above the knee, in the left forearm, below the outer corner of his left eye, in the side, and in the back; he was slashed in the right leg below the knee with a saber, and he was wounded on the top of his head with the butt of a musket.

Retaliation

Mangas Coloradas gathered the warriors of his band together to discuss retaliation against the Mexicans. Although Apache bands operated independently, they would join together with other bands to assist each other when necessary. It was clear that the massacre at Janos had to be addressed, but Mangas Coloradas's band couldn't do this alone. Since Geronimo's loss had been so great, the council of warriors chose him to solicit the help of other tribes. The first band Geronimo approached was the Chiricahua, who lived in the Chiricahua Mountains. There, he met with Cochise, who called a council of warriors and invited Geronimo to speak. The Chiricahua warriors decided to join the war party, reasoning that if the Mexicans were not punished for the massacre, they might be emboldened to attack other Apache at will. After arranging for the Chiricahua to join him in about four months, Geronimo moved on to solicit the help of the Nednai, who were his wife's people. They agreed to join the force against the Mexicans.

Key Apache Chiefs

Two Apache chiefs played significant roles in Geronimo's life: Mangas Coloradas, chief of the Bedonkohe Apache, and Cochise, chief of the Chiricahua, who were frequently allies of the Bedonlohe. Mangas Coloradas (Red Sleeves) was born around 1795 in the mountains of present-day Cochise County, Arizona. He was a very tall man. He had two Native American wives, and when he was about twenty-five, he took a captured Mexican woman as a third wife. He became chief of the Bedonkohe in 1837. The Mexican government had placed a bounty on Native Americans, and the previous chief was killed along with other Apache men, women, and children by a group of trappers for a payment. In revenge, Mangas Coloradas and his warriors slaughtered trapping parties, people on supply trains heading to the region, and local citizens of Santa Rita, thus clearing the area of white and Mexican inhabitants. During the Mexican-American War, Mangas Coloradas offered to assist the American troops, but the offer was turned down. He arranged for one of his daughters to marry Cochise, forming an alliance with the Chiricahua. Although he and his tribe were continuously at war with the Mexicans, he was at peace with the Americans until the gold rush of 1848 led to thousands of white people pouring into Apache land. On January 17, 1863, an aged

This work by Angus MacBride shows Mangas Coloradas leading an Apache band.

Mangas Coloradas was captured. While he sat by the fire in the camp, one of the soldiers stabbed him in the leg with a bayonet. When Mangas Coloradas jumped up, the soldiers that were guarding him fired their guns at him, killing him and claiming he was trying to escape. It was revealed they were acting under the orders of Colonel J. R. West, the commanding officer in charge of his arrest.

Cochise was the leader of the Chiricahua Apache. Not much is known about his early life. Cochise maintained a positive relationship with the Americans until the "Bascom Affair" of 1861, when he was wrongly accused of kidnapping the stepson of an Arizona rancher and stealing the rancher's cattle. Following his arrest and escape, Cochise conducted raids against white settlers and fought US troops. He avoided capture by hiding in the Dragoon Mountains. In 1872, he made an agreement for a reservation on Apache land, saying, "The white man and the Indian are to drink of the same water, eat of the same bread, and be at peace." He died in 1874. Warriors of his tribe painted his body red, yellow, and black, then buried him in the Dragoon Mountains. The exact location of his grave is unknown, but the area in which he was buried is called Cochise's Stronghold.

At the appointed time, hundreds of Apache arrived in the secluded valley that had been chosen to keep the gathering of warriors secret. Many of the soldiers who had killed Geronimo's family were members of a force stationed in the town of Arizpe, in Sonora. The Apache decided to make their attack there. The women and children were hidden where they would be safe. The Apache then divided into three groups. The Mimbreño and Bedonkohe were led by Mangas Coloradas, Cochise led the Chiricahua, and the Nednai were under the direction of their leader, Juh. When they reached the valley where Arizpe was located, the group chose Geronimo to lead the fighting, despite the fact that he was not a chief. In his autobiography, Geronimo attributes this decision to the fact that he had been the most seriously wronged. Geronimo was determined to live up to the trust that had been placed in him. In his first test of military strategy, he stationed the warriors in the mountainous area to the east of the town, where they couldn't be seen. He used a small party of warriors to lure a few soldiers from the town and kill them. He knew that when they didn't return, the inhabitants of the town would assume they had been killed. The next morning, the troops stationed in the town rode out. The Apache were ready and attacked in force. The ensuing battle lasted two hours. Geronimo fought with such ferocity that when he was spotted by the Mexicans, they shouted "Watch out! Geronimo!" No one knows exactly what they meant, but some experts think they were calling on St. Jerome for protection. The name stuck. The Mexicans continued to refer to him as Geronimo, and eventually the nickname was adopted by the Native Americans as well.

After two hours, Geronimo killed the last of the soldiers. After the battle, the Apache warriors surrounded Geronimo and appointed him war chief of the Apache. The position of war chief was equivalent to "general," not to overall chief of a tribe.

After the battle, the other Apache were satisfied that vengeance had been exacted for the massacre. Geronimo, however, wanted further revenge. After several months, he persuaded two warriors, Ahkochne and Kodehne, to accompany him back into Mexico. Taking three days' rations with them, they walked into Mexico from the north, and followed the Sierra de Antunez Mountains south until they came to a small village. They attacked the village, but the Mexicans were armed with guns and opened fire from their houses. The two warriors accompanying Geronimo were killed. Geronimo was surrounded by Mexicans three times, but according to his autobiography, he kept "fighting, dodging, and hiding," as he retreated toward Arizona. Mexicans mounted on horses tried to capture him, but he continued to run and hide. After two days, he succeeded in getting away from his pursuers. Although his attack on the village was a debacle, he was still determined to kill more of the hated Mexicans. About two months after his first ill-fated attack, he recruited two more warriors to join him in an attack on another village. One night, they camped near the village they planned to attack, but in the morning, they saw Mexican troops riding toward the mountain range where the Apache people lived in Arizona. Abandoning their original plan, they followed the troops instead. Three days later, the Mexican troops reached Geronimo's village. They

Geronimo meets with General George Crook in 1886.

opened fire, killing three small boys. Many of the warriors were away at the time, but the ones who were in or near the camp, including Geronimo, succeeded in driving the Mexicans out of the mountains. As the Mexicans rode south toward Mexico, four warriors followed them to ensure they left Arizona.

After the successful defense of the village, Geronimo was able to get a larger group of warriors to follow him. A short while after the attack on his village, Geronimo and twenty-five warriors followed the path the Mexican troops had taken into Mexico. They ambushed a company of cavalry troops who were walking single file, at a point where they had to make their way through a mountain pass, and killed them all. Even though they had won, so many Apache warriors were lost in the battle that they didn't go on the warpath again for a year.

As Geronimo grew older and gained more experience, he became more selective about his targets and planned his attacks better. He began to lead successful raids, aided by his growing reputation as a warrior. For example, in the summer of 1862, he led a small band of Apache warriors once again into Mexico. This time, they camped in an area where mule trains passed, laden with goods. When one came by, they attacked. The four mule drivers ran for their lives as soon as they observed the Apache, abandoning the mule train. The Apache collected the goods and the mules and returned home. Instead of reproach for a failed endeavor, Geronimo was greeted with a feast.

This time, they were prepared for retaliation from the Mexican troops as well. They sent out scouts to watch for soldiers approaching the camp, and all their warriors were present. When the scouts eventually spotted Mexican troops, the Apache were prepared. They killed ten soldiers, and the rest retreated, with Apache warriors following them until they were back in Mexico. Throughout the 1860s, Geronimo continued to lead war parties on raids into Mexico, each time returning with booty.

The Apache Wars

The Bascom Affair, described earlier, led to twelve years of fighting between the US military and a coalition of Cochise's and Mangas Coloradas's Apache. Geronimo frequently participated in the raids. The Apache acquired rifles through illegal trading with Americans by ambushing soldiers, and by capturing army pack-mule trains laden with guns and ammunition. Geronimo was an expert shot, and his favorite weapons were the Springfield 1873 and Winchester 1876 rifles.

The Apache Wars culminated with the Battle of Apache Pass in July 1862, during the Civil War. The battle took place between the Apache warriors and the Union volunteers of the California Column, which was on the march from California with the intent of capturing Confederate Arizona and then reinforcing New Mexico's Union army. The Californians had just captured a Confederate fort in western Arizona. They planned to march east, through Apache Pass, Arizona, en route to New Mexico. The commander, Colonel James H. Carleton, sent a column of soldiers ahead in advance of the main force. The advance column, led by Captain Thomas L. Roberts, reached Apache Pass on July 15. About two-

Geronimo (*in front*) and Chokonen Apache Chief Naiche (*mounted*) with a band of warriors in Mexico

In 1887, Geronimo posed for a photographic portrait with his rifle.

thirds of the way through the pass, the American force was ambushed by approximately five hundred Apache warriors, led jointly by Mangas Coloradas and Cochise. Geronimo says in his autobiography that he fought in the battle. After a short fight, Roberts and his men withdrew to the mouth of Apache Pass. They set up mounted artillery guns (called howitzers) in the pass, and Roberts ordered his troops to capture the hills above the pass. The Apache had built stone breastworks there, which protected them from some of the howitzer fire. By nightfall, they were forced to abandon their positions. The Apache came back the next morning but were forced to retreat again when the howitzers opened fire. In the wake of the battle, the army established Fort Bowie at Apache Pass. The fort was manned by one hundred rank-and-file infantrymen and California Volunteers.

Hell's Forty Acres

In 1871, President Ulysses S. Grant sent a peace delegation to the Arizona Territory and established a reservation system for the Apache. The reservations were administered by four agencies in Arizona and one in New Mexico. By the 1870s, American occupation of Arizona and New Mexico made it apparent that the Apache had no choice but to make some degree of accommodation with the Americans if they wanted to survive. The Chiricahua, Bedokohe, and other Apache tribes agreed to settle on two reservations in their tribal homelands. By doing so, they hoped to allow their children to retain their traditional way of life but live in peace. In 1872, Cochise signed a peace treaty with Brigadier General Oliver O. Howard, thus ending twelve years of fighting between the Apache and the Americans. The treaty established the Apache Pass reservation, which encompassed the Sulphur Springs Valley, Dragoon Mountains, and San Pedro Valley. Seven hundred Chokonen, Nehnhi, and Bedokohe settled on the reservation. The Tularosa reservation in New Mexico housed another 544 Chiricahua Apache.

A mere four years later, Cochise died, and the US government reneged on its agreement. It wanted the Apache Pass area for white settlement and mining. The government announced that all of the Native Americans on the Apache Pass reservation would be relocated to the San Carlos Apache Indian Reservation. The land of the San Carlos reservation was poor, and the conditions under which the Apache lived were deplorable. It was known by both whites and Apache as "Hell's Forty Acres."

About one third of the Chiricahua, who wanted to live in peace regardless of the cost, agreed to move to the San Carlos reservation, which they did under military escort. The remaining two thirds fled to the Sierra Madre Mountains of northern Mexico and resumed their raiding. Geronimo was among the latter group, leading about four hundred Chiricahua into Mexico. The US government branded the Apache who refused to live on the reservation "hostiles."

In 1873, the Apache settlement in the Sierra Madre was attacked by Mexican troops. The Apache defeated them. In retaliation, they decided to carry out raids against the Mexicans. They packed up all their belongings, and the whole tribe moved into Mexico, making camp in the mountains near Nacori, in the Mexican state of Sonora. The Apache spent a year raiding Mexican settlements. Mexican troops discovered them, and the Battle of White Hill ensued. The warriors and troops marched toward each other, meeting about 5 miles (8 km) from the Apache camp. Both the Apache and the troops took cover behind rocks. The Mexicans shot at the Apache but couldn't hit them while they remained under cover. The Apache killed a few Mexicans with arrows, but to do any real damage, they decided they would have to charge the troops. Geronimo made a sign for the warriors to advance, and with a war-whoop, they attacked and began fighting the troopers hand-to-hand. The sudden attack took the troopers by surprise, and the Apache killed all who didn't run away. Over the next decade, the Apache continued to move back and forth between the mountains of Mexico and Arizona.

In 1877, John Philip Clum, the Indian Agent for the San Carlos Apache Indian reservation, captured Geronimo and a group of his followers. Geronimo was placed in chains and taken to the San Carlos reservation for the first time. Living conditions were terrible, and the land was unfit for agriculture, so the Apache were dependent on the government for provisions. In addition, the various Apache bands had to live with the fact that all Apache were the same to the US government. In fact, the different subtribes had separate traditions and cultures. Geronimo and the other Chiricahua did not get along with some of the other tribes. With Chief Victorio of the Warm Springs band of the Tchihendeh, Geronimo started a resistance movement against being forced to live on a reservation. Geronimo and his followers would periodically escape from the reservation and attack US forces.

Never Surrender

In 1880, twenty-four Mexican soldiers attacked a camp that Geronimo and about forty warriors had set up in a forested area of the mountains south of Casa Grande. The troops surprised the Apache, killing two before the Apache could respond. Geronimo led the warriors stealthily through the forest until they were within 10 yards (9 m) of the soldiers. They then opened fire. Both sides shot at each other until all the soldiers and twelve of the Apache were dead. After the battle, the Apache packed up and started home, traveling to the northeast. Near Nacori, more Mexican troops attacked them. Three companies of Mexican troops and approximately eight Nednai and Bedonkohe Apache faced off in a field. The soldiers attacked. The Apache scattered, shooting back as they fled. The Apache dispersed, so there was no single target for the troops to concentrate their fire. Later, they met up in the Sierra Madre mountains and held a council, at which they decided that with the Mexican troops attacking them from all sides, it was time to make peace with the Mexicans in Casa Grande.

Approximately four months later, the Apache met with the leaders and men of the town of Casa Grande and agreed to a peace treaty. The Mexicans gave them an alcoholic beverage called mescal. Because they were not used to alcohol, the Native Americans quickly became drunk. While they were incapacitated, Mexican troops rode in from another town and attacked, killing twenty of the Apache and capturing others. The remaining Apache fled.

This photo shows a glimpse of what life was like on the reservation in Arizona.

After the treachery at Casa Grande, the Apache returned to the San Carlos reservation. Unable to adjust to life on the reservation, Geronimo and a band of warriors (and their families) returned to Mexico in 1883, staying in the mountains and fighting Mexican troops. They remained for about fourteen months and returned to Arizona in 1884 in order to recruit more warriors to their cause. The soldiers in Arizona chased them down, and they lost fifteen warriors without being able to gain more recruits. They again made camp in the mountains of Mexico, but US troops followed them from the north, while Mexican troops sought them from the south. They tried moving south so that they would face only one set of troops. The Mexican troops attacked. The fight lasted all day, with heavy losses on both sides. In his autobiography, Geronimo says he was hiding in a ditch where he could overhear the general in charge of the troops. According to Geronimo the general said, "Yonder in those ditches is the red devil Geronimo and his hated band. This must be his last day. Ride on him from both sides of the ditches; kill men, women, and children; take no prisoners; dead Indians are what we want." Geronimo shot the general. The response was a hail of bullets from the troops, but Geronimo wasn't hit. The fighting continued until night. In the darkness, Geronimo and the remaining Apache escaped to the mountains. This was Geronimo's last battle against the Mexican army.

From that time on, the US Army was trying to capture Geronimo. At one point, five thousand troops (almost one-quarter of the army's forces at the time) were attempting to find and capture him. On September 4, 1886, Geronimo finally surrendered to General Nelson Miles in Skeleton Canyon, Arizona, which is just north of the Mexican border. He signed a treaty with the general. Geronimo and about four hundred other Apache were transported by train to Fort Pickens, Florida, where they were to remain as prisoners. They were subsequently moved to the Mount Vernon Barracks in Alabama, and ultimately, in 1894, to Fort Sill, in the vicinity of Lawton, Oklahoma. Geronimo was held for more than fourteen years at Fort Sill. He was such a celebrity, however, that people would come to the fort, trying to catch a glimpse of him. Because of his popularity, he was occasionally allowed to appear at world's fairs and other events. He died still a prisoner in 1909 and was buried at Fort Sill in the new state of Oklahoma. On his deathbed, he said, "I should never have surrendered. I should have fought until I was the last man alive."

A lithograph portrait of
Geronimo from 1907

Hero or Villain?

Chapter Four

There is no doubt that the Native Americans were badly treated. The Europeans and Americans took their land, disrupted their way of life, and forced them onto reservations. Today, Geronimo is often viewed as a fearless warrior who fought for years against the Mexicans and Americans who threatened his people. He was a larger-than-life figure, whose fearlessness and ruthlessness were recognized in his own time and whose reputation has endured to the present day. His exploits and ability to escape capture for years are legendary. It's not accidental that since World War II, US paratroopers have adopted the cry "Geronimo!" when jumping into danger.

The Victors' View

Prior to his capture, a picture of Geronimo as a demon was popularized by both the press and military commanders. The goal of neither was to provide a realistic or balanced view of Geronimo. In the late 1880s, in articles in southwestern papers, Geronimo and his band were referred to as "fiends," "red devils," "savage villains," "butchering barbarians," "murderous wretches," and "savage beasts." The national press wasn't exempt from demonizing Geronimo and the Apache. For example, the May 23, 1885, issue of the *Chicago Tribune* featured a story with the headline "A Trail of Blood—Geronimo and His Band of Chiricahua Bucks Begin the Work of Murder—Half a Dozen Miners and Settlers Already Massacred by the Fleeing Indians."

The press wanted to sell newspapers. The more dramatic the portrayal, the more the public was likely to want to read about Geronimo. The military officers wanted to rev up their men. By painting Geronimo in the worst light possible and emphasizing his attacks on the civilians the soldiers were sworn to protect, the stories appealed to soldiers' sense of honor and assuaged any guilt they might feel about killing him and other Apache, convincing them of the rightness of killing Native Americans. Demonic depictions of Geronimo also made it clear to soldiers that they had better find and kill the monster before he slaughtered them.

As with many historic figures, Geronimo's actions have been reinterpreted as time has passed and values have changed. The Geronimo of the nineteenth century was seen by the US government and the US Army as a brutal savage who remorselessly killed both soldiers and civilians, and who kept hostilities alive long after other Native Americans had agreed to peace. General Nelson Miles, to whom Geronimo surrendered in 1886, said of the attitude of the US government, "Every one at Washington had now become convinced that there was no good in the old chief, and he was, in fact, one of the lowest and most cruel of the savages of the American continent." Even at that time, however, some military officers had a certain grudging admiration for Geronimo, given his prowess and determination to do whatever was necessary for the survival of his people. In his memoirs, General Miles says of his first meeting with Geronimo, "He was one of the brightest, most resolute, determined-looking men that I have ever encountered." Townspeople in the American Southwest and Mexico were terrified of him when he was free. At the same time, they were fascinated by him. Once he was captured, people would travel to Fort Sill, where he was imprisoned, to view the famous warrior. In his later years, he was allowed to make appearances at state fairs.

Decades after Geronimo died, parents still warned their children, "If you don't behave, Geronimo will get you." As Winston Churchill said, "The victors write the history books." According to one historian, in the early to mid-1900s, many Army veterans and family members wrote books about the Apache, including both memoirs and novels. Although they noted some of Geronimo's admirable qualities, such as his courage and energy, they portrayed him primarily as a ruthless savage who couldn't be trusted and who committed atrocities against white settlers and soldiers.

Dix-Neuvième année. — N° 963 | Huit pages : CINQ centimes | Dimanche 21 Juillet 1907

Le Petit Parisien

TOUS LES JOURS
Le Petit Parisien
(Six pages)
5 centimes

CHAQUE SEMAINE
LE SUPPLÉMENT LITTÉRAIRE
5 centimes

SUPPLÉMENT LITTÉRAIRE ILLUSTRÉ

DIRECTION: 18, rue d'Enghien (10e), PARIS

ABONNEMENTS

PARIS ET DÉPARTEMENTS :
12 mois, 4 fr. 50. 6 mois, 2 fr. 25
UNION POSTALE :
12 mois, 5 fr. 50. 6 mois, 3 fr.

EN AMERIQUE
Un Meeting d'Apaches révoltés dans l'Arizona

A newspaper illustration depicts the Apache planning a revolt against the US government.

Geronimo's exploits were so astounding and so well covered by the newspapers of the day that even while he was still alive, they were already providing the grist for popular fiction. Charles King, who was an officer in the 5th Cavalry before becoming a novelist, wrote fifty novels set on the military frontier in Arizona. His novels were written from the perspective of the brave soldiers fighting in the American West, and they portrayed Geronimo as a bloodthirsty villain. Other novels from the early twentieth century did this as well, including *Trailing Geronimo*, written by Edward S. Ellis in 1908, Everett T. Tomlinson's 1920 novel *The Pursuit of the Apache Chief*, and *When Geronimo Rode*, written in 1924 by Forrestine C. Hooker. The works of the period inevitably portrayed the conflict as that of primitive savagery represented by the Native Americans, and civilization represented by the white men.

In 1886, the magazine *Harper's Weekly* sent artist Frederic Remington to Arizona as a correspondent and illustrator to cover the US government's war with Geronimo. Remington never managed to see Geronimo in person, but he created many paintings of the American West, most of which featured Native Americans. Again, he portrayed the US troops as the heroes of the day. Many people in the East formed their opinion of Native Americans from Remington's illustrations, in which the soldiers were often shown at an advantage over their Native American counterparts. For example, in one illustration, "Indian Scouts on Geronimo's Trail," Remington showed an officer flanked by Native American scouts assisting him. The officer cuts a dashing figure on a fine horse, but the scouts are scrawny specimens on foot wearing only loincloths.

This view is just as distorted as those that portray Geronimo as a heroic freedom fighter, whose actions were justified by the crimes against his people perpetrated by white men and Mexicans. The army's version of events reveals as much about the officers who were his enemies as Geronimo himself. It represents the soldiers' view of the implacable enemy they faced, but not the way that the Apache saw him. Even among the Apache, views about Geronimo were divided. There were those who saw him as a great leader that fought the Americans who threatened them, but other Apache—especially in the latter days of the Apache Wars—viewed him as a reactionary and a disruptive force, who upset their attempts to live a peaceful life and enticed young warriors to join him on pointless raids that got them killed.

A more humane view of Geronimo came from Edgar Rice Burroughs, who is most well known for having written the *Tarzan* series of books and the *Martian Tales,* including *John Carter of Mars*. Prior to becoming a writer, Burroughs had been a private in the 7th Cavalry and had pursued Apache in the 1890s. He attempted to write a trilogy about the Apache that featured Geronimo as the adoptive father of an orphaned white boy, whom he raises as an Apache. Burroughs wrote only the first two books, *The War Chief* (1927) and *Apache Devil* (1933), which were originally serialized in *Argosy* magazine and later published as books. He never wrote the third installment because he got fed up with the magazine's criticism of his positive portrayal of the Native Americans. In the books, Geronimo wants to live in peace but is repeatedly forced to take to the warpath because of the white men's misdeeds.

Burroughs's sympathetic approach to the Apache was carried on by other writers, however. Will Levington Comfort's *Apache* (1931) told the story of Mangas Coloradas, and Paul I. Wellman's novel *Broncho Apache* (1936) is about an Apache who escapes from Geronimo's prison train and makes his way back to the West, with soldiers in pursuit. Wellman's book became the film Apache in 1954. In 1947, Elliott Arnold wrote the novel *Blood Brother*, which describes how peace was brought to Arizona through the friendship between Cochise and US Army scout and Native American agent Tom Jeffords. The book was the basis for the movie *Broken Arrow* in 1950.

Recognition of the wrongs done to Native Americans increased from the mid-twentieth century on, as the public gained a greater understanding of the motivations for the Native Americans' attacks on the whites in the West. The tone in fiction first became more sympathetic to their plight and later supportive of their actions. During the era of the Vietnam War, the Apache were sometimes used as a symbol of resistance to a foreign power invading one's land. In Hunter Ingram's novel *Fort Apache* and Robert Vaughan's *Savages,* Geronimo desires peace but has no choice but to wage war because of the actions of whites determined to kill Apache. Forrest Carter's 1978 novel *Watch for Me on the Mountain* features Geronimo as a tough warrior who also has mystical shamanistic powers. By the early twenty-first century, Geronimo had switched from being a villain to being the hero in fiction. Beginning in the 1950s, Elmore

An 1888 illustration by Frederick Remington shows Geronimo and his band returning from a raid into Mexico.

Leonard wrote western short stories. This excerpt from the back cover blurb of his *Trail of the Apache and Other Stories* (2017), a collection of his early western stories, captures the change of view toward Geronimo and other Native Americans: "Destiny, restlessness, and greed moved the white man west, into lands occupied for centuries by a proud and noble people: Arapahoe, Navajo, Apache, Sioux."

Only a decade after Geronimo's death, however, his qualities of courage, determination, and strength were beginning to coexist with the image of him as ruthless and bloodthirsty. The Atchison, Topeka, and Santa Fe Railroad named a railroad car after him. When William C. Allen decided to open a plant in Enid, Oklahoma, to manufacture automobiles in 1917, he dubbed the enterprise the Geronimo Motor Company, which produced a car called, naturally, the Geronimo.

Geronimo on Display

After their capture, Geronimo and his followers were initially imprisoned in Florida. The people in the eastern United States had never experienced the brutality of the Apache raids or attacks on civilians. To them, the name Geronimo took on legendary proportions, whether as a famous warrior who had fought courageously for his people or a bloodthirsty savage who had evaded capture for years. At Fort Pickens in Pensacola Bay, Florida, the captive Apache were a tourist attraction. When they were moved to Mobile, Alabama, in May 1888, the Pensacolian newspaper lamented the fact that their "Big Injun, and large-sized curiosity Geronimo" was being moved. The phrasing of this complaint goes a long way toward showing the contemptuous way that the Native Americans were viewed. Geronimo was not seen as a human being, but as a curiosity, like a trained tiger in the circus. Some of the people who came to see him complained he was too mild-mannered. They wanted to see a wild man who butchered people, not an ordinary man.

In 1894, the Apache were again moved, this time to Fort Sill in Oklahoma, because many of them had caught tuberculosis in the Deep South. Geronimo continued to be a celebrity. On the outskirts of the fairgrounds of the 1898 Omaha Exhibition, Geronimo was featured along with other Native Americans, who demonstrated to the fairgoers how they lived, dressed, and danced. At the 1901 Pan-American Exposition in Buffalo, New York, Geronimo was displayed as a sideshow exhibit. Even though he was now elderly, he was still accompanied by a US Army guard to make sure he didn't escape. The Indian Wars, as they were then called, were turned into a spectacle, with mock Native American vs. cavalry skirmishes performed three times a day for visitors. At the 1904 St. Louis Louisiana Purchase Exposition, more commonly called the St. Louis World's Fair, Geronimo was exhibited in a tepee as part of the ethnology exhibit. He sold autographs for ten US cents (about $2.75 today) and photographs for two US dollars (about $55.00 today). The exhibit's organizer, S. M. McCowan, thought Geronimo's prices were high, "but then he is the only Geronimo." Some might think Geronimo was being exploited. However, he not only enjoyed being in the limelight but accrued money from his public appearances.

The Atkinson, Topeka, and Santa Fe Railroad's Geronimo train car.

After the fair, Pawnee Bill's Wild West Show worked out a deal with the US government for Geronimo to become a member of the show. He continued to travel under Army guard. According to the Smithsonian, "The Indians in Pawnee Bill's show were depicted as 'lying, thieving, treacherous, murderous' monsters who… would think nothing of taking a scalp from any member of the audience." Visitors came to ogle the "savage," and they paid for a button from his coat. He earned a significant amount of money from traveling with the show, and he also acquired money by playing poker with soldiers at the fort. According to the Smithsonian, he used some of his money to educate the Apache children. When he died, he left an estate worth several thousand US dollars (a thousand US dollars then was the equivalent of around $27,000 today).

His greatest triumph as a celebrity was being invited to participate in President Theodore Roosevelt's inaugural parade in March 1905. Geronimo and five Native American chiefs rode horses along Pennsylvania Avenue in Washington, DC. Geronimo met with Roosevelt and tried to convince him to let the imprisoned Apache return to Arizona, but Roosevelt refused.

Geronimo's View

In 1906, Geronimo wrote an autobiography, dictating it to a schoolteacher through an interpreter. Geronimo considered the range of mountains near the head of the Gila River in Arizona (where he was born) his homeland. In his autobiography, he says, "Among these mountains our wigwams were hidden; the scattered valleys contained our

Pawnee Bill (*left*) and Buffalo Bill Cody (*right*) ran popular Wild West shows.

fields; the boundless prairies, stretching away on every side, were our pastures; the rocky caverns were our burying places." As a child, he was taught that Apache pray to their god Usen for help with many things: strength, health, wisdom, and protection—but they did not ask Usen to smite their enemies for them. Usen, it was said, did not care for the petty disagreements of men. If an Apache was wronged, it was up to him to take vengeance. The penalty for Apache who didn't pull their weight—who were lazy, cowardly, or untrustworthy—was exile. Offenders were forced to leave the tribe, and no other tribe would accept them. They were left on their own in a hostile environment. Sometimes, several outcasts joined together, forming an outlaw band. Such bands were small, and the result of an attack was usually the death of the outlaws. For a tribal people, ostracism was a terrible—and possibly fatal—punishment. Young people learned to embody the values that were important to the survival of the tribe, such as courage. Geronimo grew up hearing of the brave deeds of Apache warriors, and success in war was glorified. When he was seventeen years old, he was admitted to his tribe's council of warriors, which meant he could fight alongside the other warriors. In his autobiography, he says: "The customs of our tribe prohibited me from sharing the glories of the warpath until the council admitted me. When opportunity offered, after this, I could go on the warpath with my tribe. This would be glorious. I hoped soon to serve my people in battle."

These values clashed with those of the American soldiers and settlers in some ways, but in others, they were very similar. The soldiers with whom Geronimo so often clashed also believed that there was honor in defending their people, the Americans who had settled in the region. They also believed in avenging attacks against their people. Thus, the two groups—Apache and soldiers—were doomed to conflict by their shared values as much as their differences.

Geronimo often engaged in unprovoked attacks on Mexican villages or troops, but the Mexicans also engaged in attacks on the Apache villages. When they (either group) did so, they sometimes captured women and children, whom they kept as slaves, making the captives work for them. When the Mexicans captured Apache men, they kept them confined in chains. In contrast, according to Geronimo, when the Apache captured men, they made them "cut wood and herd horses," but they didn't chain or imprison them as the Mexicans did with the Apache. The Apache attempted to integrate women and children captives into the tribe.

Honor was a significant motivation for Geronimo. It was considered a disgrace to return to the Apache camp from a raid with no booty, especially if any warriors had been killed in the attack. Great honor was associated with being successful on the warpath, bringing back goods that were necessary to sustain the tribe. An unsuccessful raid meant that the warriors had to endure the taunts and criticism of their peers. Honor also demanded not letting the enemy gain the advantage. For this reason, in 1865, when Mexican troops stole all the tribe's horses and mules from an area near the camp, Geronimo led a party of warriors that followed them to a ranch where they corralled the animals. They attacked and killed the men guarding them, and they took the stock back.

When reading about the raids carried out by the Apache, it's easy to see them as "lawless savages." At the time Geronimo lived, the Mexicans and white men of the West behaved in an equally lawless manner, however. Both white men and Mexican troops disregarded the law, attacking Native American camps, stealing their goods, and killing or taking captive the women and children. They did not restrict their attacks to Native Americans. The Mexican and white men were just as brutal when attacking other Mexicans and whites in order to steal their money or goods. It was an environment in which there was no regular civil police force. It was every man for himself, and survival meant being willing to fight.

Geronimo was often angered by the behavior of the US forces toward his people. In his autobiography, he described what he felt was the greatest wrongdoing to the Apache by the US Army: In 1863, the chief of the Apache, Mangas Coloradas, went to the white settlement at Apache Tejo, New Mexico, because the Apache had heard that the people there could be trusted to live up to their treaties. At a council attended by Mangas Coloradas, three Apache warriors, local citizens, and US Army soldiers, Mangas Coloradas was told that if he brought his tribe to live near the settlement, the US government would supply them with blankets, food, and other supplies. Mangas Coloradas agreed to return with the tribe in two weeks. When he got back to the Apache settlement, he called a council of the entire tribe. Geronimo didn't believe the white people in the settlement could be trusted. Nonetheless, the council decided that Mangas Coloradas should return to Apache Tejo with part of the tribe. If the settlers kept to the terms of the treaty, the rest of the tribe would join them, and they would settle permanently at Apache Tejo. Geronimo was designated to lead the part of the tribe that stayed behind. Still dubious, the Apache who stayed behind gave most of the tribe's weapons and ammunition to the group going to Apache Tejo, so that they would be prepared in case of treachery. The group that went to Apache Tejo was never heard from again. Eventually, the Apache who stayed behind heard that Mangas Coloradas's group had been captured and killed.

Uncertain as to how to react, the remaining Apache hid in the mountains near Apache Pass. To acquire provisions to sustain them while they were in hiding, they killed four men moving a herd of cattle through the mountains and took the cattle. While they were butchering the cattle and packing the meat, they were attacked by US troops who killed a number of Apache, including three women and three children. The rest fled into the mountains. They regrouped at a site about fifty miles (80 km) from the attack. They were attacked twice more by US troops. Eventually, the soldiers gave up trying to kill the remaining Apache and headed back toward the San Carlos reservation.

It's difficult to say who was in the wrong. The white men lured the Native Americans to their death by treachery, and the Apache attacked innocent cattle herders to get the food they needed to survive—which they wouldn't have needed if the US troops weren't determined to trap and kill all the Apache.

A year later, just as winter was setting in, US troops again made a surprise attack on the Apache settlement. They killed four men, five women, and seven children, took all their supplies, and burned their tepees. With winter coming on, Geronimo's tribe needed provisions. Geronimo managed to get provisions from Chief Victoria of the Oje Caliente Apache, a tribe in New Mexico, with whom he was friendly. The Bedonkohe Apache stayed with Victoria's tribe for a year.

Apache-American Hostilities

In his memoirs, Geronimo claimed that the Apache tried to live in peace with the white soldiers and settlers, but the soldiers were treacherous, making trouble for the Apache and committing misdeeds against them. He accused the soldiers of reporting the attacks made by the Apache but never admitting to their own acts of bad faith. For example, about a year after making a peace treaty with the Bedonkohe and Chokonen Apache, who were under the leadership of Cochise, Mangas Coloradas and other Apache were invited by officers of the US Army to come to a conference at Fort Bowie at Apache Pass. When they arrived, the Apache were ushered into a tent. There, they were attacked by soldiers. Mangas Coloradas and some other warriors escaped by cutting through the tent wall. Many of the warriors were killed or captured. A few days later, the Apache returned to Apache Pass, intent on fighting the soldiers. They skirmished with them for a few days and then attacked a freight train bringing supplies to the fort. They captured some men and offered to trade them for the warriors whom the soldiers had taken prisoner. When the soldiers refused, the Apache killed the captives and returned to the mountains, where they hid. After this incident, the Apache never trusted US

Sitting Bull

Geronimo was far from the only Native American leader associated with resistance against the US government. Among the most prominent was Sitting Bull, chief of the Lakota Indians, located in the Dakota Territory. Sitting Bull was born in 1831 on land that would later become South Dakota. He had little contact with white people until 1862, when Native Americans who were defeated in the Santee Sioux uprising in Minnesota were forced to move to the western plains. Sitting Bull learned from them how bad life on a reservation was, and he became determined to keep his people from being forced onto one.

In 1863, General Alfred Sully led an attack against a Native American camp on Killdeer Mountain. Sitting Bull fought in the camp's defense, and the Native Americans won the Battle of Killdeer Mountain. After the battle, to avoid further trouble with US troops, Sitting Bull joined with other Sioux leaders in moving his people to the valleys of the Powder and Yellowstone Rivers. In 1868, he was chosen as chief of the Lakotas. Sitting Bull's rejection of treaties with the US government and his refusal to agree to live on a reservation gained him a large number of followers from Sioux, Cheyenne, and Arapaho tribes.

A large community of Native Americans built a village on the Little Bighorn River. At a Sun Dance ceremony there in 1876, Sitting Bull had a vision of

President Theodore Roosevelt greets a Native person during a visit to Canada.

defeating the US Army. In June 1876, he led his forces against those of General George Armstrong Custer in the Battle of Little Bighorn, where Custer and his men were wiped out. The US government was embarrassed by the loss, and the Army redoubled its attempts to gain control of the Dakota Territory. Sitting Bull took his people to Canada to evade the US troops and stayed there for four years. They had a hard time surviving without the herds of buffalo that they relied on for food. In 1881, Sitting Bull brought the near-starving tribe back to the Dakota Territory. He was captured and held prisoner for two years.

In 1885, Sitting Bull met sharpshooter Annie Oakley and became a member of Buffalo Bill Cody's Wild West Show. He eventually grew tired of performing and dealing with the negative attitude of the audiences toward him as a Native American. Declaring, "I would rather die an Indian than live a white man," he returned to his people, residing in a cabin on the Grand River. In 1889, Sitting Bull joined other Native Americans in practicing a ceremony called the Ghost Dance, whose purpose was to get rid of the white people in the territory and bring back the Native American ways. The authorities were afraid that Sitting Bull's involvement in the movement would lead to trouble, so they had Lakota police officers arrest him. They dragged him out of his cabin and shot and killed him in the ensuing gunfight.

Army troops again. They agreed among themselves not to befriend the white men. The result was a constant conflict in which the soldiers sometimes attacked the Apache, and the Apache sometimes attacked the white men.

Native American Resistance

To many people, Geronimo represents determined resistance to invaders who sought to take his homeland from his people. He was a believer and defender of traditional Apache values, including the nomadic life, which became increasingly difficult as more and more American settlers claimed the land through which the tribes had once traveled freely.

The Apache were a meritocracy. Their chiefs did not inherit their positions. They were elected because they had achieved the respect of their peers. This meant showing great skill and courage. Geronimo's exploits against the Mexicans and US forces earned him respect and eventual elevation to a tribal leadership position. When white settlers and soldiers flooded into Apache territory after the Mexican-American War ended in 1848, Geronimo opposed the idea that Mexico had the right to give the Apache's homelands to the Americans—and that the Americans had the right to take the Apache's lands from them.

Geronimo was the embodiment of single-minded armed resistance, despite the overwhelming odds. Many of his fellow Apache disagreed with his approach. In the 1870s, the US government forced the Apache to move to reservations far from their tribal homelands. They were escorted to these reservations by US troops, and it became clear to many Apache that the US government had more troops than they

This illustration depicts the capture and death of Native American chief Sitting Bull.

could defeat. Many understood that adopting the white man's way of life was the only way they could live in peace and survive. For these Apache, Geronimo's attacks on US soldiers merely stirred up trouble and brought retaliation upon them, interfering with their attempts to live peaceably with the white population. In other words, Geronimo's activities only made their situation worse. Many also felt that Geronimo was still acting out of a desire for revenge for the death of his family decades earlier, and that in this sense, he was mentally unbalanced.

Changing Times

By the 1880s, many Apache had come to the conclusion that the Americans were unlikely to be driven out of their territory. They saw no point in engaging in strikes against them that would simply result in more deaths of Apache warriors. Young Apache, who were the most inexperienced warriors and the most likely to be killed, particularly embraced this viewpoint. This attitude would have shamed Geronimo in his youth, but things were different as the century approached its end. The Apache had become familiar with the ways of the settlers and had found ways to engage in trade with them. Weapons had changed, too. Prior to the arrival of the white men, war was carried out with bows and arrows and knives. By the 1880s, rifles were the weapons of choice. Although people could be killed from a distance with arrows, a hail of bullets could be fired from a distance faster and often with deadlier results. Since the American settlers were widespread and impossible to drive out, there seemed no point in dying in a futile effort to resist them.

Many Apache just wanted to get on with their lives in peace, even if it meant living on the reservation.

Victorio, chief of the Warm Springs band of Apache, was killed by Mexican troops in October 1880. Geronimo volunteered to lead a war party back to San Carlos to free his Warm Springs followers from the reservation there. At that time, they were led by Loco, a chief of the Mibreno band. Geronimo wanted to free as many warriors as possible in order to increase his manpower, but not all the Apache wanted to join him. Many just wanted to live in peace or thought attack was futile. When some of Loco's band hesitated, Geronimo reputedly ordered his followers to shoot any who refused to go. The group hid in the mountains of northern Mexico. They were ambushed by Mexican soldiers, and a deadly battle ensued. Seventy-eight Apache were killed, most of them members of Loco's band. Thirty-three women were captured, including Loco's daughter. Most of the Warm Springs band held Geronimo responsible for their losses, because he had forced them to leave the San Carlos reservation, where they had been safe. Loco hated Geronimo, who he felt had kidnapped rather than rescue his band. Chief Vittorio's daughter, who was a member of the White Springs band, represented the viewpoint of some of the younger Apache. She felt that Geronimo's headlong approach to warfare resulted in the death of too many young, inexperienced warriors and believed he was more interested in his own glory than the welfare of the Apache.

To many white settlers and soldiers, Geronimo was a cruel savage. He killed not just soldiers but also innocent men, such as cowboys moving cattle, in order to steal livestock or goods. This image was supported not only by his incredible ferocity in battle, but also by the indifference he showed toward killing civilians. The Apache's scalping of victims was also interpreted by the white man as torture or savagery. In reality, the Apache primarily scalped other warriors, both Native Americans and soldiers. The practice served two purposes: it disheartened the enemy warrior, who, if he survived, bore a humiliating mark of having lost in battle, and it allowed the warrior to prove, on his return to camp, how many enemy warriors he had defeated. In this way, the practice was similar to taking a body part, such as an ear or finger, from the bodies of enemy soldiers to make a body count, as has occurred from time to time in wars in the Balkans, Korea, and Vietnam. The practice has been generally disapproved of, but keeping track of the dead enemy is a way to "keep score" in situations where the military is not allowed or able to capture and hold enemy land. This is not to excuse Geronimo's behavior, but merely to counteract the idea that he was unique or berserk. The fact is that the Mexican soldiers, US troops, and Native American warriors all committed atrocities. They all attacked innocent civilians, including women and children. The Native Americans burned towns, and the Mexicans and Americans burned Native American villages, but the Americans didn't describe themselves as crazed savages when they wrote their memoirs. All parties demonstrated the remarkable ability of human beings, be they Native American, Mexican, or white, to see only their own people as "human." Other groups who differ in skin color or language have always been seen as "less human" and therefore expendable, especially in times of war.

Time Heals All Wounds

In the nineteenth century, the brutal attacks inflicted by Geronimo and his followers struck terror into the hearts of the soldiers and settlers alike, on both sides of the Mexico-America border. They were more concerned about their own survival than with the wrongs done to the Native Americans. The era of the Indian Wars ceased with the end of the nineteenth century. Time and distance eventually altered the public's view of Geronimo. The negative image of Geronimo didn't begin to change until people began to understand—or, perhaps more accurately, began to care about—the ways that the Native Americans had been abused by the American and Mexican governments and military. The first acknowledgment of the wrongs done to the Native Americans was brought to the public's consciousness just after the Civil War—while Geronimo was still active—by abolitionists William Lloyd Garrison and Wendell Phillips. After the conclusion of the Civil War, Garrison and Phillips turned their attention from the wrongs done to African Americans to the atrocities committed against the Native Americans. Thus, the violence committed by Native Americans, such as Geronimo, was shown in a new light.

Novelists began to write stories that featured Geronimo as a hero instead of a villain, a courageous warrior fighting for his people. As writers brought to the public's attention the wrongs that had been done to the Native Americans, many people developed a sense of guilt or at least an understanding that the native population of America had not been treated fairly. In this light, it became possible to understand Geronimo's anger and to see him as a man who, if not always fighting for his people's rights, was certainly avenging the misdeeds done against them. His actions could be viewed as resistance to the white attempts to destroy his land and culture. From the mid-twentieth century to the present, there has been an increasing awareness of the value of Native American culture, and it has become less acceptable to discount and take advantage of people because of their ethnicity. As societal attitudes have changed, the public has come to view Native American leaders such as Geronimo, who defied the people invading their land, as protectors of their people rather than villains. This view, however, can be taken just as far to the extreme as the view of Geronimo as a brutal savage. It ignores the fact that Geronimo did kill innocent people in order to take the goods his people needed. In this sense, Geronimo saw only his people as important, just as the white soldiers saw only the white people as important.

Embracing this revisionist view of Geronimo, in 1993, the US government issued a postage stamp in Geronimo's honor. In February 2009, the US House of Representatives passed a resolution declaring that Geronimo, who was portrayed as a bloodthirsty villain for decades, was a "spiritual and intellectual leader" who "led his people in a war of self-defense."

The truth is that Geronimo is not easily defined. He was a complex individual who could show great courage, determination, and tactical skill, but also self-interest and ruthlessness. He possessed a combination of characteristics that suited him well for survival in the turmoil of the nineteenth-century West. Geronimo was not only intelligent and determined, he was also adaptable. As times changed, he changed too, defying the ability of people to define him by a few simple characteristics. It was a long journey from the angry, headstrong young warrior to the calm old man. On one hand, Geronimo possessed courage, resourcefulness, a sense of honor, and loyalty to his people. On the other hand, he was ruthless, killing without remorse, when it was necessary to obtain resources or to take revenge against the nearest target, even if the people he killed weren't the ones who had committed the wrongs. In short, he was a human being with a complex personality, and the ability to call on the traits that would be most beneficial in a given situation. When survival required war, he was a warrior. When it required living in the white man's world, he became a performer.

Native Americans took over Alcatraz in 1969 to protest their treatment. They chose Geronimo as one of their symbols.

Geronimo's Influence

Chapter Five

Even during his own lifetime, Geronimo was a larger-than-life character who captured the public's imagination, and his reputation has been growing ever since. His personality and actions have had an effect on both entertainment and social consciousness. Geronimo's biggest influence was not on American history, but on American culture. He became a symbol used in art, literature, film, and television—first representing the cruel savage, then the fearsome warrior, and finally the leader of resistance in the face of oppression. From his own time to the present, more than a hundred years later, Geronimo remains a powerful image.

Geronimo in Popular Media

In American culture, Native Americans have typically been stereotyped as either treacherous, bloodthirsty monsters or "noble savages"—pure primitive people, uncorrupted by civilization, who live in harmony with nature (a view popularized by novelist James Fenimore Cooper). These images of Native Americans permeate literature, painting, photography, and film, and have influenced generations of Americans. The stereotype of the bloodthirsty savage was certainly prevalent in Geronimo's day. It persisted into the mid-twentieth century, when it was replaced in the 1960s and 1970s, to a large extent, by the noble savage stereotype.

The depiction of Geronimo and Apache culture in early Hollywood westerns promoted and reflected the prevailing negative cultural ideas about the Native Americans. Since 1903, over seven thousand westerns have been filmed by the American film industry, and that number doesn't take into account the thousands of episodes of television westerns that have been made since the 1940s. The formula for the western was established early in the history of film: a superior white hero prevails over a vicious or treacherous Native American. The stereotypical vicious Native American was often an Apache, because of their reputation for cruelty and unrelenting warfare. It's worth noting that in the early westerns, Apache were frequently portrayed as more vicious and violent than Native American tribes that lived on the Plains, such as the Cheyenne and Sioux. This image of Apache culture was influenced no doubt by the portrayal of Geronimo in both contemporary newspaper accounts and the memoirs and novels of the 1890s and the early twentieth century. Dramatic versions of their attacks and atrocities would have been familiar to people at the beginning of the twentieth century, and early filmmakers made the most of this fact.

Geronimo died in 1909, and by 1912, a movie about him was produced, *Geronimo's Last Raid.* The plot revolves around the capture and escape of Geronimo, but the film is essentially a romantic adventure: Geronimo is a supporting character to the central story, which focuses on the character of Parker, but it is made clear that Geronimo is a savage villain.

In *Stage Coach*, a movie directed by John Ford in 1939, a coach traveling through Arizona receives a warning that Geronimo is leading a band of Apache on the warpath. Geronimo's name alone is enough to send the characters into a panic. The film was a success and encouraged the production of other westerns featuring fearsome Apache. Another Geronimo-based film produced in 1939 was the appropriately named *Geronimo.* The story focuses on a feud between a father and son who are both officers during the army's attempt to capture Geronimo and his band of rampaging warriors. In the 1930s, movie studios typically sent promotional packets to movie theaters with suggestions on how they could promote the movie. In this case, Paramount suggested that theater managers play sound effects such as Native American war drums and war cries. The studio's advertising posters promoted Geronimo as "The Most Feared Warrior Who Ever Ravaged the West!" Geronimo was a nonspeaking part and, according to a *New York Times* film

In the 1962 film *Geronimo*, Chuck Connors portrayed the titular character in a sympathetic light.

reviewer on February 8, 1940, he had two expressions: "grim and grimmer."

According to Paramount's publicity department, the film was responsible for the adoption of "Geronimo!" as the battle cry of paratroopers. The studio spread the story that at Fort Benning, Georgia, paratroopers had watched the movie before a test jump and had then cried "Geronimo!" when jumping. All five airborne divisions adopted the battle cry in World War II, embracing Geronimo's image of ferocious courage. In 1941, the 501st Parachute Infantry Battalion added Geronimo's name to its insignia patch. On the eve of D-Day, many of the paratroopers of the 101st Airborne Division cut their hair into Mohawks and applied war paint to their faces, adopting the warrior tradition of Geronimo.

After World War II ended, the Apache were again portrayed as savage enemies in two westerns directed by John Ford, *Fort Apache* in 1948 and *Rio Grande* in 1950. Both films were based on short stories by James Warner Bellah, who portrayed the Apache in an extremely negative way. Geronimo was shown to be a villain, even when other Native Americans received a more balanced treatment. Attitudes toward minorities were beginning to change, however. The civil rights movement agitated for equitable treatment of blacks and an end to segregation, and this mindset led some people to reevaluate the treatment of other minorities, such as Native Americans. In *Broken Arrow* (1950), Cochise is treated as a sympathetic character, although Geronimo is still a villain, whom Cochise considers as much as a threat to the peace as the white men are. Films made by Hollywood that promoted black civil rights often faced a negative public reaction. Some filmmakers used westerns as a vehicle to promote the idea of racial justice, substituting Native Americans for blacks. The fact that *Broken Arrow* was a commercial success led Hollywood to make other movies that showed a more humane view of Native Americans. In the film, Geronimo was played by Jay Silverheels, who portrayed the Lone Ranger's Native American sidekick, Tonto, in the 1950s television series.

The positive portrayals of Native Americans in films from the 1950s to the 1970s didn't keep television shows of the period from recycling the traditional concept of the bloodthirsty villainous Native American in a long list of television westerns. After 1960, the popular portrayal of Geronimo in movies switched from negative to positive.

In the 1950s and 1960s, a new methodology for studying different cultures emerged. This approach, called ethnohistory, combines anthropology and history. Researchers use a blend of historical sources and knowledge of the culture of the people being studied to answer both anthropological and historical questions. The result is an interpretation of the subject of peoples' historical behavior in terms of their culture, rather than as a series of facts colored by the viewpoint of the people doing the studying. By the second half of the twentieth century, ethnohistory became the major approach to studying other cultures. The understanding of the Apache and other Native Americans produced by this approach

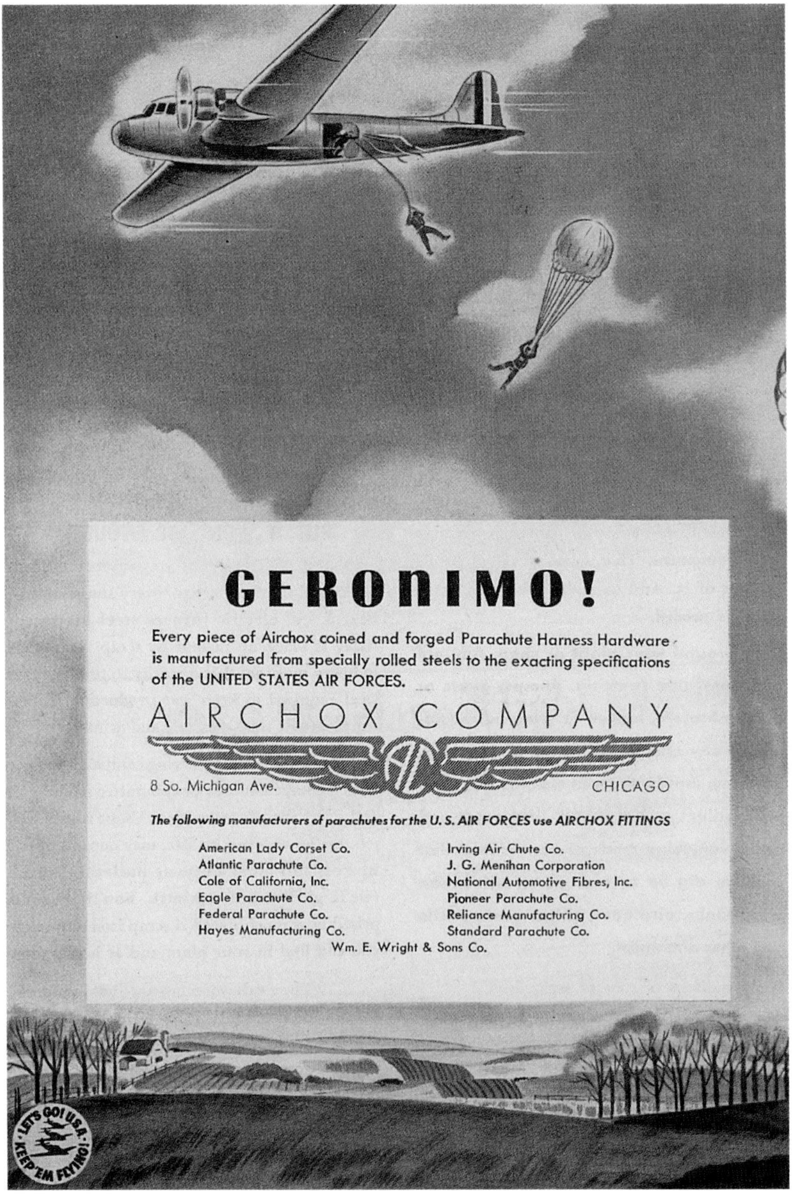

This ad from the 1940s capitalizes on the adoption of the cry "Geronimo!" by US paratroopers.

colored the way that Native Americans were portrayed in the media.

Hollywood started to show Geronimo defending the Native American people against the white invaders who sought to usurp their rights. An example is the 1962 movie *Geronimo*, in which Chuck Connors plays Geronimo as a man who modifies his warrior ways in order to obtain peace for his people. Geronimo was portrayed as a similarly doomed hero in a variety of television shows from the 1970s through the 1990s, including Mr. Horn, "The Last Apache" episode of *Gunsmoke*, *Geronimo*, and the PBS *American Experience* episode called "Geronimo and the Apache Resistance." A sign of the changing attitude is the description of 1993's *Geronimo: An American Legend* in the Internet Movie Database (IMDB): "The story of the Apache chief and his armed resistance to the US government's subjugation of his people."

Geronimo as a Symbol of Resistance

The interaction between Native Americans and the US government has been one of constantly changing policies. There was the policy of the US government in the late nineteenth century that Native Americans, including the Apache, were to be removed from their lands to reservations, so that whites could settle there unopposed. There was the policy by which Native Americans were to be forcibly assimilated (i.e., made to live like white people). This policy was characterized by, for example, the removal of Apache children from reservations in the early twentieth century, in

A Native American group altered this sign on Alcatraz Island when they took it over in 1969. They claimed that the 1868 Fort Laramie Treaty gave them the right to reclaim it.

order to send them to the Carlisle Indian Boarding School in Pennsylvania, where they were taught the ways of the whites.

The coercive assimilation policy was reversed in 1932, when John Collier was appointed Commissioner for Indian Affairs. Collier supported tribal restoration, established by the Indian Reorganization Act of 1934. The goal of this policy was to preserve Native American tribes, both culturally and legally.

In 1978, President Jimmy Carter signed into law the American Indian Religious Freedom Act, which protects Native American rights to the land on which their religious rites and ceremonies are traditionally performed. The act was controversial because the Native Americans' desire to protect certain sites conflicted with commercial interests' desire to develop them. This is illustrated by the mid-2010s controversy over running the Keystone Pipeline for oil over Native American land.

By the 1970s, Native Americans had observed and learned from the civil rights movement. College-educated Native American social activists began to organize protests, and in 1968, the American Indian Movement (AIM) started in Minneapolis-St. Paul, Minnesota. AIM engaged in protests and occupations. In 1969, AIM carried out a widely publicized occupation of Alcatraz Island, near San Francisco, home to the then-closed prison of the same name. Today, tours of the island include artifacts of the occupation, which have been respectfully preserved by the National Park Service. During the AIM occupation of Alcatraz, an 1884 photograph of Geronimo was included on the placard that the organization put in place. Geronimo had become the poster child for the resistance fighter who stands up to injustice against his people—not merely a symbol for Native Americans, but a symbol of resistance in general. Social activist and Black Panther Party leader Elmer Pratt adopted the name Geronimo ji-Jaga in a similar gesture of resistance. Bobby Sands, a prominent member of the violent revolutionary organization the IRA (Irish Republican Army) in the late twentieth century, was known to sign himself "Geronimo" at times.

Geronimo was a complex individual who lived a long life, and went through major transitions, both as a person and in terms of his image. The modern view of Geronimo is that he was a hero of Native American resistance to the white invaders who attempted to usurp his lands and destroy his people's way of life. The older image persists of Geronimo as a savage, wreaking destruction on white settlers and instilling terror in the population. When US Special Forces mounted their successful operation to kill notorious al-Qaeda terrorist Osama bin Laden, they named their operation "Geronimo." They weren't using the name as a battle cry on that occasion. During the operation, they referred to bin Laden by that name, as in "Geronimo has been sighted." The choice of Geronimo's name for the operation resulted in objections and criticism from offended Native Americans who view Geronimo as a hero of their people.

The various uses of Geronimo's name show how hard it is to eliminate negative images, as well as how the view of Geronimo has changed over time. To the pioneers and settlers of Arizona and New Mexico, Geronimo was a bloodthirsty killer, and this was the dominant view until the second half of the twentieth century. To the Apache, however, Geronimo possesses true Apache values, including fierceness in battle and courage in the face of adversity.

Historian Eve Ball, who pioneered the oral history of Native Americans in the 1940s and 1950s, interviewed Chiricahua Apache on the Mescalero reservation in New Mexico. One Apache she interviewed said of Geronimo, "I don't think he wanted to kill, but there were cases where he had no choice. If he were seen by a civilian, it meant that he would be reported to the military and they'd be after us. So, there was nothing to do but kill the civilian and his entire family ... But the soldiers killed our women and children too. Don't forget that." Kanseah, Geronimo's nephew, who was mentored by Geronimo from the time he was eleven, describes the obstacles that Geronimo faced and overcame: "Geronimo had to obtain food for his men, and for their women and children. When they were hungry, he got food. When they were cold, Geronimo provided blankets and clothing. When they were afoot, he stole horses. When they had no bullets, he got ammunition. He was a good man."

annex To attach or add to existing territory.

assimilate To be absorbed into.

atrocity A horrible, cruel, or brutal act.

aura Atmosphere.

Black Panther Party An African American revolutionary organization active from 1966 to 1983.

cartel A coalition of people with a common interest.

confiscate To seize goods, usually done an government authority.

debacle A disastrous failure.

deplorable So awful as to cause disapproval.

encroachment The movement of one group of people into another's territory.

exposition A fair at which art, cultural artifacts, and/or manufactured products are displayed, such as a world's fair.

flux Continuous change.

homogeneous To be all alike.

Glossary

incapacitated Unable to act or respond.

incendiary Likely to cause a flare up of violence.

indiscriminately Without making any distinctions between people or objects.

influx The streaming in of people or material.

melee A chaotic fight.

mesa A flat-topped hill.

nomadic People who move from place to place continuously rather than settling in one place.

ostracize To banish from a community.

Paleolithic people People who lived from about 50,000 to 10,000 years ago. Those who reached the Americas did so close to the end of the Stone Age.

prowess Skill.

reactionary Taking a very conservative view, as opposed to a progressive or forward-looking one.

renege To go back on one's word or an agreement.

retaliation An attack or punishment in revenge for a wrong done.

1829

Geronimo is born in No-Doyohn Canyon in present-day New Mexico.

1840s

Geronimo becomes a warrior and marries his first wife, Alope.

1848

The Mexican-American War ends with the Treaty of Guadeloupe Hidalgo. The United States gains the territory including New Mexico and Arizona.

1858

Geronimo's entire family is killed by Mexican troops while he is on a trading expedition near Janos, Mexico.

1861

The Bascom Affair occurs, leading to twelve years of warfare between the Apaches and US troops.

1863

Mangas Coloradas, the chief of Geronimo's tribe, is captured and killed by US troops.

Chronology

1872

The US government establishes the Chiricahua Apache Reservation in southern Arizona.

1876

The US government moves the Apaches on the Chiricahua Reservation to the San Carlos reservation in Arizona. Geronimo refuses to go and escapes.

1880

The people of Casa Grande, Mexico trick Geronimo into coming to the town to sign a peace treaty and attempt to kill him and his followers. Geronimo returns to the San Carlos reservation.

1886

Geronimo surrenders to General Nelson Miles at Skeleton Canyon in southern Arizona. He and his followers are sent to Florida as prisoners of war.

1905

Geronimo rides in President Roosevelt's inaugural parade. He tells the story of his life to S. M. Barrett, and the book is published as *Geronimo: His Own Story*.

Books

Ball, Eve. Indeh: *An Apache Odyssey*. Norman, OK: University of Oklahoma Press, 1988.

Cozzens, Peter. *The Earth Is Weeping: The Epic Story of the Indian Wars for the American West*. New York: Random House, 2017.

Geronimo and S. M. Barrett. *My Life*. New York: Dover Publications, 2005.

Treuer, Anton. *The Indian Wars: Battles, Bloodshed, and the Fight for Freedom on the American Frontier.* Washington, DC: National Geographic, 2017.

Websites

First People: Geronimo His Own Story
http://www.firstpeople.us/FP-Html-Legends/Geronimo_His_Own_Story_1d.html#Tribal_Amusements_Manners_and_Customs

Excerpts from Geronimo's autobiography are provided, which shed light on the culture of the Apache as well as Geronimo's personal experience.

Further Information

Fort Bowie

https://www.nps.gov/fobo/index.htm

This site, run by the National Park Service, includes information on the fort at Apache Pass that played a central role in the Apache wars; the site also features information on the Chiricahua Apache.

Fort Sill Apache Tribe

https://fortsillapache-nsn.gov

This is the official website of the Chiricahua and Warm Springs Apache tribe, whose members are descended from those who fought with Geronimo and were imprisoned with him at Fort Sill; it provides a historical and cultural information on the tribe.

Indian Country Today

https://indiancountrymedianetwork.com/history/people/know-the-real-geronimo-life-of-native-american-hero-photos

This Native American–run site tells the story of Geronimo illustrated by numerous photographs.

PurpleHawk's Apache Photo Gallery

http://www.impurplehawk.com/apgallery2.html

This site has collected an impressive array of period photographs of the Apaches, including Geronimo.

"Apache." Encyclopedia Britannica, accessed November 1, 2017. https://www.britannica.com/topic/Apache-people.

Ball, Eve. *Indeh: An Apache Odyssey*. Norman, OK: University of Oklahoma Press, 1988.

Brookeman, Christopher. "The Native American Peoples of The United States." *American Studies Today* Online, accessed November 25, 2017. http://www.americansc.org.uk/Online/brookman.htm.

Clements, William M. *Imagining Geronimo: An Apache Icon in Popular Culture*. Albuquerque, NM: University of New Mexico Press, 2013.

Drye, Willie. "Seven Cities of Cibola." *National Geographic*, accessed November 2, 2017. https://www.nationalgeographic.com/archaeology-and-history/archaeology/seven-cities-of-cibola/.

Flavin, Francis. "Native Americans and American History." National Park Service, accessed November 25, 2017. https://www.nps.gov/parkhistory/resedu/native_americans.pdf.

"Geronimo." Biography.com, accessed November 1, 2017. https://www.biography.com/people/geronimo-9309607.

Selected Bibliography

Geronimo and S. M. Barrett. *Geronimo: My Life*. (unabridged reproduction of original 1906 book) Mineola, New York: Dover Publications, 2005.

"Geronimo: Ruthless Apache Chief." Warfare History Network, February 6, 2017. http://warfarehistorynetwork.com/daily/military-history/geronimo-ruthless-apache-chief.

"Geronimo: The Good or the Wicked?" Myths of the American West, November 13, 2015, https://mythsoftheamericanwest.wordpress.com/2015/11/13/geronimo-the-good-or-the wicked.

Hansen, Matthew. "Hansen: Glory from Omaha's 1898 world's fair was fleeting." *Omaha World Herald*, February 8, 2014. http://www.omaha.com/news/hansen-glory-from-omaha-sworld-s-fair-was-fleeting/article_edbbc8c4-d10f-5239-a9bf-c5eaf198b6bc.html.

History.com staff. "Geronimo." History.com, accessed November 1, 2017. http://www.history.com/topics/native-american-history/geronimo.

———. "The Mexican-American War." History.com, accessed November 6, 2017. http://www.history.com/topics/mexican-american-war.

———. "Treaty of Guadalupe Hidalgo." History.com, accessed November 1, 2017. http://www.history.com/topics/treaty-of-guadalupe-hidalgo.

Hocking, Doug. "The Alleged Bascom Affair." *True West*, July 21, 2015. https://truewestmagazine.com/the-alleged-bascom-affair.

Hutton, Paul Andrew. *The Apache Wars: The Hunt for Geronimo, the Apache Kid, and the Captive Boy Who Started the Longest War in American History.* New York: Crown Publishing, 2016.

———. "Was Geronimo a Terrorist?" *True West*, July 28, 2011. https://truewestmagazine.com/was-geronimo-a-terrorist.

King, Gilbert. "Geronimo's Appeal to Theodore Roosevelt." Smithsonian.com, November 9, 2012. https://www.smithsonianmag.com/history/geronimos-appeal-to-theodoreroosevelt-117859516.

"Mangas Coloradas." Encyclopedia Britannica, accessed November 19, 2017. https://www.britannica.com/biography/Mangas-Coloradas.

"Mangus Colorado." Native American Nations, accessed November 19, 2017. http://www.nanations.com/warriors/mangus_colorado.htm.

McLachlan, Sean. *The Apache Wars: The History and Legacy of the U.S. Army's Campaigns Against the Apaches.*

CreateSpace Independent Publishing Platform, Charles River Editors, 2015.

Memmott, Mark. "Native Americans Offended By Code Name 'Geronimo' In Bin Laden Mission." National Public Radio (NPR), May 4, 2011. https://www.npr.org/sections/thetwo-way/2011/05/04/135985017/native-americansoffended-by-codename-geronimo-in-bin-laden-mission.

"On This Day: Old Apache Indian Chief Geronimo Is Dead (obituary). *New York Times*, February 18, 1909. http://www.nytimes.com/learning/general/onthisday/bday/0616.html.

"President McKinley and the Pan-American Exposition of 1901." Library of Congress, accessed November 14, 2017. https://www.loc.gov/collections/mckinley-and-the-pan-american expo-films-1901/articles-and-essays/president-mckinley-and-the-panamerican exposition-of-1901.

"Sitting Bull." History.com, accessed November 21, 2017 http://www.history.com/topics/native-american-history/sitting-bull.

"Sitting Bull: Warrior, Military Leader (1831–1890). Biography.com, accessed November 21, 2017. https://www.biography.com/people/sitting-bull-9485326.

Sonnichsen, C. L., ed. *Geronimo and the End of the Apache Wars*. Lincoln, NE: University of Nebraska Press, 1990.

Page numbers in **boldface** are illustrations.

Index

About the Author

Jeri Freedman has a Bachelor of Arts degree from Harvard University. She worked for a number of years in the education department of the Anti-Defamation League in programs providing information on the Holocaust to history teachers. She is the author of more than fifty young adult nonfiction books, including *Tech in the Trenches: Strategic Inventions of World War II*, *Tech in the Trenches: Strategic Inventions of the Napoleonic Wars*, and *A Documentary History of the Holocaust: The Warsaw Ghetto and Uprising*. She is the coauthor, under the name Ellen Foxxe, of two alternate-history fantasy novels.